W9-CHR-064

Super Structures

One World Trade Center

Dash!
LEVELED READERS

An Imprint of Abdo Zoom • abdopublishing.com

3

Dash!
LEVELED READERS

Level 1 – Beginning
Short and simple sentences with familiar words or patterns for children who are beginning to understand how letters and sounds go together.

Level 2 – Emerging
Longer words and sentences with more complex language patterns for readers who are practicing common words and letter sounds.

Level 3 – Transitional
More developed language and vocabulary for readers who are becoming more independent.

abdopublishing.com

Published by Abdo Zoom, a division of ABDO, PO Box 398166, Minneapolis, Minnesota 55439.
Copyright © 2019 by Abdo Consulting Group, Inc. International copyrights reserved in all countries.
No part of this book may be reproduced in any form without written permission from the publisher.
Dash!™ is a trademark and logo of Abdo Zoom.

Printed in the United States of America, North Mankato, Minnesota.
052018
092018

Photo Credits: iStock, Shutterstock
Production Contributors: Kenny Abdo, Jennie Forsberg, Grace Hansen, John Hansen
Design Contributors: Dorothy Toth, Neil Klinepier

Library of Congress Control Number: 2017960595

Publisher's Cataloging in Publication Data

Names: Murray, Julie, author.
Title: One World Trade Center / by Julie Murray.
Description: Minneapolis, Minnesota : Abdo Zoom, 2019. | Series: Super structures | Includes online resources and index.
Identifiers: ISBN 9781532123122 (lib.bdg.) | ISBN 9781532124105 (ebook) | ISBN 9781532124594 (Read-to-me ebook)
Subjects: LCSH: World Trade Center Site (New York, N.Y.)--Juvenile literature. | National monuments--Juvenile literature. | Architecture--building design--Juvenile literature. | Structural design--Juvenile literature.
Classification: DDC 720.48309--dc23

Table of Contents

One World Trade Center

One World Trade Center
is in Lower Manhattan,
New York. It stands near
where the Twin Towers
were once located.
They were destroyed
in a terrorist attack on
September 11, 2001.

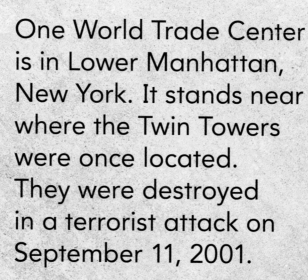

The building is often called the Freedom Tower. It is part of the World Trade Center complex. The complex is a **symbol** of hope and a bright future.

9/11 Memorial & Museum

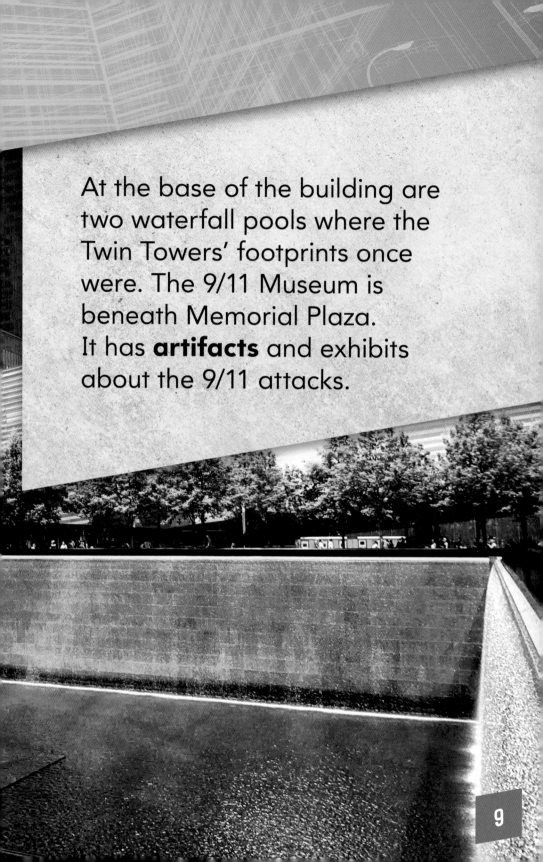

At the base of the building are two waterfall pools where the Twin Towers' footprints once were. The 9/11 Museum is beneath Memorial Plaza. It has **artifacts** and exhibits about the 9/11 attacks.

The Building

One World Trade Center is made of **concrete**, steel, and glass. More than 45,000 tons of steel was used. More than 210,000 cubic yards of concrete was used. That is enough to make a sidewalk from New York to Chicago!

Construction began in April 2006. It was completed in July 2013 and opened in November 2014. It cost about $3.9 billion to build.

The building has a **geometric** design. The base and top are squares. Triangular sides form an octagon in the middle.

One World Trade Center stands 1,776 feet (541 m) high. This includes the **spire**, which is 408 feet (124 m) tall.

There are 104 floors and 71 elevators. Office space takes up the majority of floors. Underground, there is shopping and access to public transportation.

One World Observatory is
on floors 100-102. There are
360-degree views of New York
City. It has exhibits, dining areas,
and a theatre.

More Facts

- One World Trade Center is the tallest building in the US. It is the sixth tallest in the world.

- The height of the building is symbolic. It represents the year 1776, which is when the Declaration of Independence was signed.

- The building is environmentally friendly. More than 40% of the material used in construction was recycled.

Glossary

artifact – any object made by human beings.

concrete – a hard, strong building material.

geometric – made up of lines or shapes like those of geometry.

spire – a tall, narrow, upward structure on the outside of a building.

symbol – an object that represents something else.

Index

Online Resources

Booklinks
NONFICTION NETWORK
FREE! ONLINE NONFICTION RESOURCES

To learn more about One World Trade Center, please visit **abdobooklinks.com**. These links are routinely monitored and updated to provide the most current information available.